the looking book

Fill this page with things you find interesting

Picture credits

Self-portrait with monkeys by Frida Kahlo, 1943
Archivart / Alamy Stock Photo

Self-portrait as Tehuana (Diego On My Mind) by Frida Kahlo, 1943
Grainger Historical Picture Archive / Alamy Stock Photo

In the Loge by Mary Cassatt, 1878
Historic Collection / Alamy Stock Photo

President Barack Obama by Kehinde Wiley, 2018
Martin Shields / Alamy Stock Photo

Red Canna by Georgia O'Keefe, 1919
Historic Collection / Alamy Stock Photo

Icarus (plate 8 from 'Jazz') by Henri Matisse, 1947
World History Archive / Alamy Stock Photo

Note from the illustrator

To explain the different styles of the artists in this book, I have tried to illustrate their techniques and ways of looking with my own artistic representations. I hope this will help you understand how they are different and see all the many ways that you can make art — there's not just one 'right' way to paint or draw, and everyone has their own style! You can use this book to explore your own.

I haven't tried to copy the work of any artists mentioned in the book, and any copying is entirely inadvertent.

PAVILION

First published in the UK in 2022 by
Pavilion Children's Books
43 Great Ormond Street
London WC1N 3HZ

An imprint of Pavilion Books Company Ltd

Text and Illustrations © Lucia Vinti, 2022

The moral rights of the author and illustrator have been asserted

Publisher: Neil Dunnicliffe
Editor: Martha Owen
Designer: Sarah Crookes

ISBN: 9781843655008

A CIP catalogue record for this book is available from the British Library.

10 9 8 7 6 5 4 3 2 1

Reproduction by Rival Colour Ltd, UK
Printed and bound by Toppan Leefung Ltd, China

This book can be ordered online at www.pavilionbooks.com, or try your local bookshop.

MIX
Paper from responsible sources
FSC® C104723

the looking book

get inspired –
see the world like an artist!

By *Lucia Vinti* and

_____

(add your name here!)

Contents

"Life moves pretty fast. If you don't
stop and look around once in a while,
you could miss it."

— Ferris Bueller, *Ferris Bueller's Day Off*

How to use this book

Our everyday world is full of exciting things — people, places, shapes, patterns, colours — but so much of it passes us by. Paying more attention to the way we look around can help us to notice more of the great things that we usually take for granted. Maybe we'll see objects and people in a different way, notice stuff that inspires us or makes us smile. Perhaps you'll see a particularly pretty puddle, a building with eyes and a mouth, a cloud that looks like a dog or a dog that looks like a cloud...

This book will help you look more closely at everything around you and explore different ways to interpret and record what you see — through drawing, painting, writing, photography and more. It's full of activities to kick-start your creativity, whether you use it at home or out and about in your surroundings. Wherever you are, look around you and be inspired to create your own style of art. Fill the pages and, most of all, enjoy!

Your toolkit

Here are a few extra things you should pop
in your bag when you go out and about.

Sketchbook or notebook
If you want more space for one of the activities or if you
get a sudden wave of inspiration, it's always good to have a
sketchbook or notebook to hand.

Phone or camera
You'll find quite a few photography
activities in this book, but if you can't get
your hands on a camera then there are
still plenty of other activities to enjoy!

Your favourite grown-up
If you're a younger artist,
make sure you have an
adult with you when
you're out and
about!

Pens and pencils
Pack your favourite supplies so that you
can draw and write on the go.

It will also be helpful to have these materials at home for some of the longer activities.

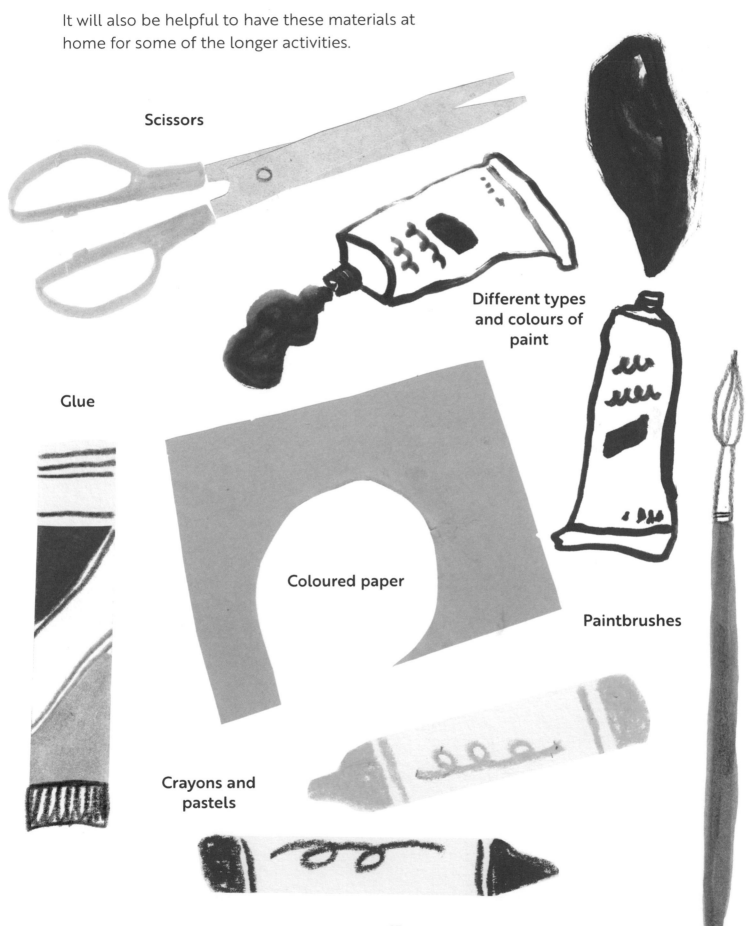

Scissors

Different types and colours of paint

Glue

Coloured paper

Paintbrushes

Crayons and pastels

At home

You can find inspiration anywhere — even when you're stuck inside! At home you can relax and experiment, finding new techniques and styles to use throughout your creative journey.

Add your own
drawings to the walls

Still lifes

A still life is where an artist draws, paints or photographs a selection of objects. Still lifes allow you to focus on looking really closely and carefully at something, so they're a great way to practise your observation skills.

Start by choosing 4–5 objects to use in your still life. Finding objects that have a wide variety of colours, shapes, sizes and textures will make your still life really interesting.

Set up the objects against a plain background with good lighting — natural daylight is always good!

The way you set up your objects will affect the composition of your picture — that's the placement of the different parts that make up a piece of art.

Some ideas for objects to include in your still life

Flowers and plants

Ornaments

Books

Fruit and veg

Jewellery and accessories

There are so many different ways to create a still life, and you can get a variety of results by using different techniques — here are a few to start experimenting with!

Continuous line drawing

Take your pen for a walk! Try and draw everything without lifting your pen from the page. You should spend more time looking at the objects than at your paper.

Negative space

Rather than focusing on the objects, look carefully at the space around them. Use black paint or a thick crayon to colour in the background, leaving the space where the objects should be blank.

Collage

Cut coloured paper to create the shapes of your objects. Start with fairly simple shapes and then layer as much detail as you'd like. Try ripping the paper for a more wibbly-wobbly result!

Drawing with a long stick

Attach a paintbrush, pen or pencil to the end of a stick using tape. Then hold the stick at the other end and draw your objects. You could even use the stick itself as a paintbrush, by dipping the end in paint or ink.

Negative space

Continuous line

Test out the techniques here

Drawing with a long stick

Collage

Clementine Hunter

1886–1988

Clementine Hunter was a self-taught artist from Louisiana in the USA. She worked on a plantation and as a housekeeper, but started painting at 53 years old when a visitor to the plantation left behind some paints. Hunter's work is often described as Folk Art or Naïve Art as she never went to art school.

Hunter painted colourful scenes based on careful observations of her daily life such as people washing clothes, going to church and farming. She painted from memory on whatever she could find, from cardboard boxes to fabric scraps and even old plates.

Create a Folk Art painting inspired by Clementine Hunter

1. The next time you're having a good day with family or friends, try to look around more than you would normally. Memorise as many details as you can, from the way things look to the way that you feel.

2. When you're home, find a surface you'd like to paint on — it could be fabric, cardboard, a bit of wood — anything goes! Make sure you are allowed to paint on it before you start your masterpiece.

3. Using a thick paintbrush and your favourite colours, paint the scene from your memory. Remember to include all of the little details that make your memory special.

Shadow play

An activity for when you're stuck inside on a sunny day. Find a patch of light where the sun is shining through the window and creating shadows. For example, maybe there is the shadow of a piece of furniture, a vase of flowers, or even just the window frame.

Hold up your book so you can see the shadows on these pages. Then draw around the shapes of the shadows. You could also fill in some of the shapes with pencil or pen to create an abstract masterpiece!

Tip!
If you can't see any interesting shadows, make your own. Cut out paper shapes and place or stick them in the window, or arrange some objects in front of the window. You could even use a torch to make shadows!

Frida Kahlo

1907–1954

For centuries, artists have used painting, drawing and photography to capture images of themselves. These are known as self-portraits. They can show what you look like, but also express how you feel and what you're thinking.

Frida Kahlo was a Mexican painter famous for her self-portraits. While she was bed-bound recovering from a bus accident, Kahlo turned to herself for inspiration and started to paint self-portraits. She completed over 50 throughout her life. Kahlo used costumes, accessories and different backdrops to explore topics such as her identity as a woman, her Mexican background and her disability.

> **"I paint self-portraits because I am the person I know best."**
>
> — Frida Kahlo

18

Create your own self-portrait

A good starting point can be to draw yourself while looking in the mirror. Like Frida Kahlo, you could think about how your clothing, facial expression and surroundings can show things about you and your personality. Remember that this piece of art is all about YOU, so make it as quirky, minimal, colourful, abstract, or realistic as you like!

Self-portrait by ——————————————————————

Now you've tackled the self-portrait, it's time to look at someone else. It can be interesting to think about the small details that make someone unique. This could be their eyes, hands, hair or even the clothes they wear. Spend some time with a friend or family member with this in mind.

Draw close-ups of their features on this page...

... and draw a full head
and shoulders portrait
of them here

David Hockney

1937–

David Hockney is a British artist who has worked in lots of different ways, from drawing on iPads to painting and photography. As an artist, he often looks closely at his surroundings and documents them in diverse and exciting ways.

Hockney created photographic collages that he called joiners. Instead of taking a single photo of his subject (which could be a place or a person) he would take lots and lots of photographs from slightly different angles. Some would be close-up and some would be from far away. Then he collaged the photos together to create one big image.

By doing this, Hockney could include lots of details that you might not see in a 'normal' photograph. Hockney could also use this technique to show movement, for example someone swimming across a pool, or even a group of friends playing a game of Scrabble!

Hockney would often create joiner portraits of still lifes.

Create your own joiner at home

1.
Choose a subject (maybe a still life with objects from your bedroom) and take as many photographs as you can.

2.
Try photos from different angles, up close and far away. Print out your favourite ones.

3.
Arrange them in different compositions on a sheet of paper.

4.
When you find your favourite composition, stick down your photos and voilà — your very own joiner!

Room with a view

Look out of your window and capture the view at four different times or on four different days

You might do this on a rainy day, a foggy day, a snowy day and a sunny day, or at morning, afternoon, sunset and night time. You'll be surprised by how much it changes! Try using different materials, like paint, pencil, crayon and collage for each picture. Think about how the material you choose reflects what you see — you could paint a drizzly day in watercolour, or maybe draw a bright pink sunset with bold-coloured crayons.

In the town

Whether you're on a day trip to the city or just wandering around your local shops, a walk in town can always have something new for you to look at and discover. Cracks in a wall can become abstract drawings, a shop sign could turn into a painting, and tall buildings are full of people's stories waiting to be told.

Fill the windows of the buildings with people, plants and decorations

Let's go for a walk!

As well as getting you from A to B, walking can be a journey all by itself, a chance to think and a opportunity to look around. Go on a walk, either to somewhere new or to a place you go every day. Use these questions and drawing prompts to record some of the things you see on your way.

Draw a house

What sounds can you hear?

Are there any shops? What are they selling?

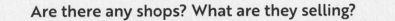

Draw a shop front

Draw a person you see

Circle all the vehicles you see

Rollerskates	Bus	Train
Bike	Motorbike	Tram
Skateboard	Car	Taxi
Lorry	Scooter	

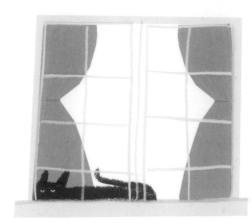

... and a window

Draw a door...

Keep count of every tree
you see. Write the total
number here

If you see a funny street name write it here!

Write down any other interesting things you spot

Draw your favourite thing from your walk

Look up!

The tops of buildings often have beautiful or interesting features that you might not usually notice. Take some time to look up, and use these pages to draw any details that you see.

Domes and turrets

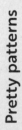

Pretty patterns

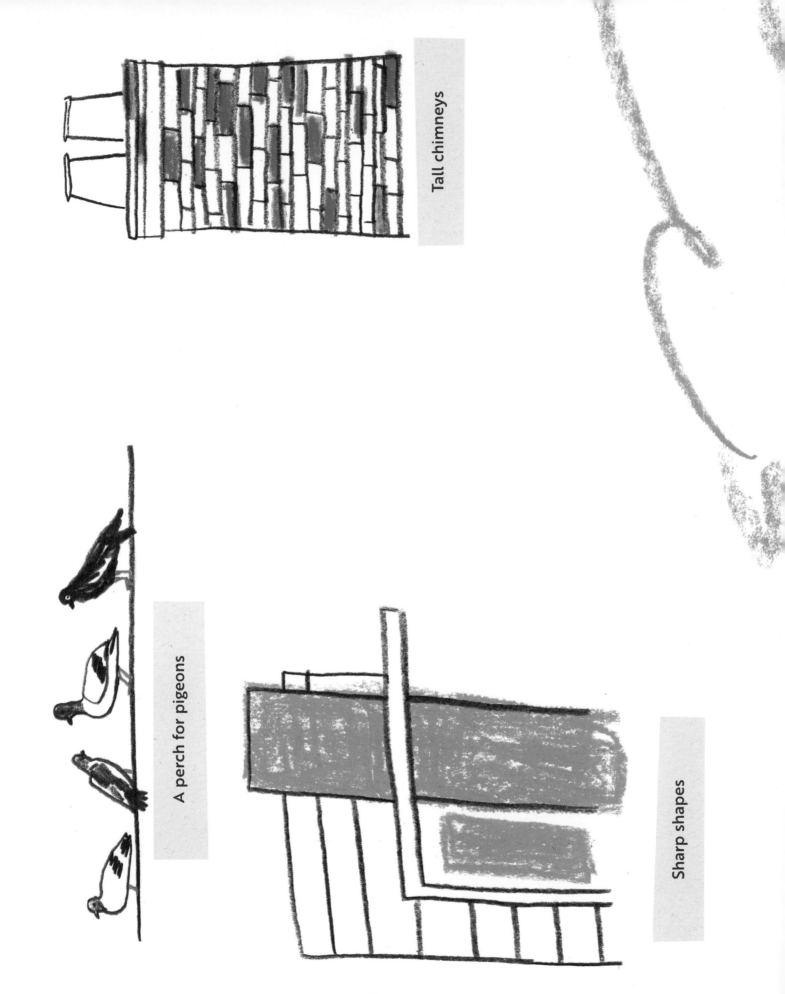

Tall chimneys

A perch for pigeons

Sharp shapes

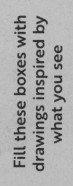

Fill these boxes with drawings inspired by what you see

Look down!

What patterns and shapes can you see on the floor? Are there any pieces of litter, colourful markings or cracks in the pavement? You could also take some close-up photographs of the floor to create abstract shapes and patterns.

Corita Kent 1918–1986

Sister Corita Kent was a nun, teacher and pop artist who made brightly coloured screen prints. Since looking closely at her surroundings was so important to her, she made a simple tool to help her students. She called it a finder, and it acts like a small portable frame that you can use to capture elements of what you are looking at.

It's easy to make your own finder, just cut out a rectangle in the centre of a piece of card and look through it. You could also try different shapes and sizes. Using a finder can help you zoom in on small details like the corner of a poster on a brick wall, or part of a busy shop front. These observations might help you to focus on interesting details and make you think differently about your surroundings.

SKETCH BOOK

How does using a finder affect the things you see on your walk? Do you notice any more interesting details? Remember to keep looking up, down, and all around!

Fill these boxes with drawings of details you spot through your finder

Now you've filled all the spaces, it's time to make a Sister Corita-inspired artwork

1. Look carefully at your favourite finder picture, and draw a bigger version of it on a piece of paper. Make sure that you fill the whole of the page with your drawing.

2. Paint or colour in your picture using three or four colours. Try and pick out the main sections of your picture and make each one a different colour.

3. Cut out the main sections of your picture.

4. Take a new sheet of paper, arrange all the cut-out shapes in a new composition and stick them down. Now you have your very own piece of pop art inspired by your observations!

Hilla & Bernd Becher
1931–2007, 1934–2015

Hilla and Bernd Becher were a husband and wife photography duo from Germany. For over 40 years, they travelled around and photographed industrial buildings and machinery — things like gas tanks, cooling towers and water towers. They took many photographs of each structure, using the same angle and lighting every time. Then they arranged the different photos into a large grid. By putting pictures of similar buildings and machines side by side, they created intriguing patterns that showed off all their similarities and differences.

It's easy to get caught up looking for beautiful or unusual things around us, but sometimes it can be good to focus on everyday things that you usually wouldn't think twice about.

Create your own photo grid inspired by Hilla and Bernd

Think of something that you see wherever you go — for example, traffic lights, benches or street signs. Every time you see a different version of the same thing, take a photograph. Then print out your photos and arrange them into a big grid. Think about what's the same and what's different in your photographs, and if seeing them together makes you look at them differently.

If you don't have a camera, you could use the same technique or tool to do a drawing each time — for example, doing a continuous line drawing with the same pencil.

While you walk through the town or city, look at all the buildings and see which ones catch your attention. Draw them here to create a street of your favourite buildings. You could draw them from real life, or take photographs to draw from when you get home.

Tip!
Think about who might be living or working in each building and draw them peeping through the windows.

43

People-watching

People-watching is a great way to spend some time on an empty afternoon and also a chance to use your imagination. For example, you can think about where each person is going, what their name might be and what their personality is like. The people you see could become characters in a story or inspire a work of art. Remember: if you're a younger artist you should always stay with a responsible adult, and you shouldn't photograph or talk to strangers!

Fill these pages with people you see in real life, in books, or from your imagination

If you spot an interesting person, imagine what their name, job and interests might be and try to memorise what they look like. When you get home, fill out one of these passports for them.

People-watching passport

Name:

Rosie

Redman

Age:

46

Portrait

Job:

Art critic and horse rider

Favourite activity:

Collecting red scarves

What are they wearing?

Red scarf, red coat, pearl earrings, black boots

People-watching passport

Name:

Age:

Portrait

Job:

Where are they going?

What are they wearing?

People-watching passport

Name:

Age:

Portrait

Job:

Favourite activity:

What are they wearing?

People-watching passport

Name:

_____

_____

Age:

_____

Job:

Portrait

_____

Where are they going?

_____

What's their favourite hobby?

_____

People-watching passport

Name:

_____

_____

Age:

_____

Job:

Portrait

_____

Where are they going?

_____

What's their favourite book or movie?

_____

People-watching passport

Name:

_____

Age:

_____

Job:

Portrait

_____

Where are they going?

_____

What's their favourite hobby?

_____

People-watching passport

Name:

_____

Age:

_____

Job:

Portrait

_____

What are they doing today?

_____

What's their favourite book or movie?

_____

What's in their bag?

Now you've imagined some interesting people, draw what you think might be inside their bags

Do you think their bag is messy or clean? Do they have top-secret documents in there, a much-loved book, a pair of running shoes? Have they got any yummy snacks, or are they carrying makeup and a change of clothes for a party? These things can help you think about what they might be like as a person and imagine what their daily life is like!

RVMAN · MVN XII

At the museum

At museums you can see anything from 10,000-year-old fossils and portraits of famous figures to ancient pots and elaborate ballgowns. No matter the type of museum, there is bound to be something that you can be inspired by. You can even visit museums from all over the world online!

Write a list of the museums you'd like to visit

Find a cool object to focus on and answer the questions below

All about _____

(title of object)

When and where is it from? _____

_____

Does it have a purpose? _____

_____

What does it look like? _____

_____

What is it made of? Can you imagine how it might feel?

_____

_____

Draw the object here!

Tip!
While you're drawing, take time to look at the shape, texture and patterns of the object. You should spend more time looking at the object than looking at your page!

Curate your own museum display!

Fill the frames with the best
pictures you see

And fill the shelves with intriguing objects

Mary Cassatt

1844–1926

Mary Cassatt was an American painter and part of a group of artists called the Impressionists. One of her most famous paintings is called *In the Loge*. The picture focuses on an opera in Paris, but instead of showing the stage, this painting is of a member of the audience — a woman looking through opera glasses. If you look closely, in the background of the painting you can also see a man looking at the woman through his opera glasses. Mary Cassatt has really made this painting all about looking!

At museums we can also see people looking at things. Take some time to watch people in the museum and think about these questions: What are they looking at? How quickly or slowly do they look at things? Do they take photos? Are they talking to anyone about what they see?

Draw some interesting people and the exhibit they are looking at

While you're at the museum,
draw something...

old

modern

patterned

with a face

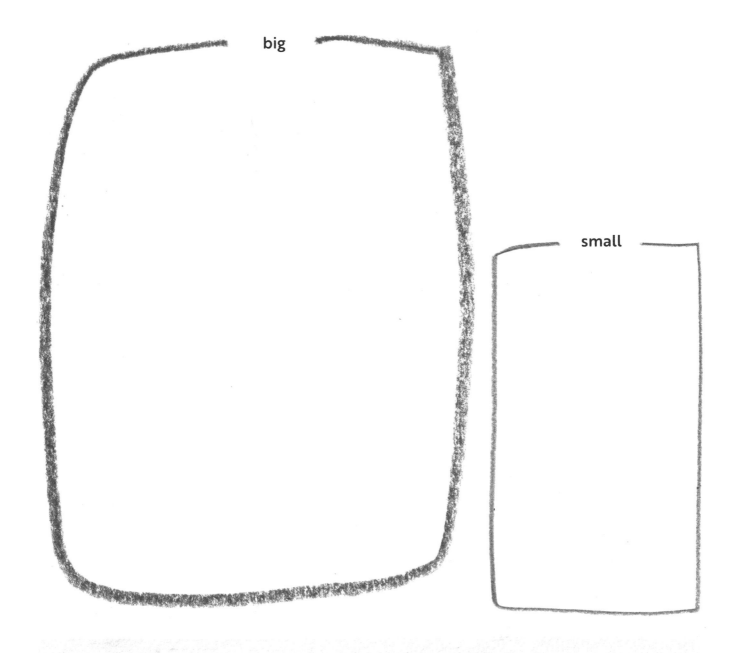

big

small

beautiful

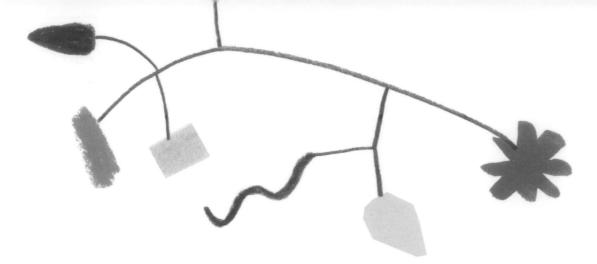

Going to the gallery

Galleries are excellent places to discover different artists and new ways of being creative. You can visit in person, or check them out online. By looking carefully at the work of other artists, you might spark ideas for your own work... Who knows, maybe your work will be in the gallery one day!

Draw some more people
looking at the art

Sometimes galleries can be overwhelming because there's so much to look at. A great thing to do is focus on just one work of art for a little while. Walk around one of the rooms and find an artwork that interests you. Fill in this guide about the picture to let someone else know about it!

All about _____

(name of artwork)

This artwork was made by _____

In the year _____

The medium is   painting   sculpture   textiles   photography

print   installation   other

I find it interesting because _____

_____

_____

_____

I think it's about _____

_____

Draw the artwork here. Take your time with your drawing, and try to pay attention to all the different details. Drawing from art in galleries can help you look at something more carefully and for longer than you might normally do.

Tip!
If the artwork seems too big or complicated to draw, you could use a finder to focus on one detail rather than the full image.

What animals can you spot throughout the gallery? Draw them here

Creative writing

Writing about art can help you understand how it makes you feel. Choose a piece of art, take some time to really look at it and answer these questions. You can start writing notes on this page, and carry on in your notebook if you need more space!

What are the colours like? Are they bright like the sun or dark as night? Are they bold and brave or are they muted and calm?

What are the shapes and textures like? Is it smooth or rough? Are the marks big or small?

What is the mood of the artwork? Does it look happy, sad, angry or peaceful? Is it loud or quiet?

Does the artwork have a meaning or a story?

Using the questions as a starting point, write a poem about the picture

You could write an acrostic poem, which is a poem where the first letter of each line spells out a word, using the title of the artwork or the artist's name. Otherwise, you could write a rhyming poem or even a short story.

Everything but the art

As well as looking at the art or objects being displayed, take time to focus on the other elements that make up the gallery.

Copy a sign or display label

Draw a fancy frame

Draw anything else that inspires you!

Draw the outside of the building

Kehinde Wiley
1977–

Kehinde Wiley is an African American portrait painter, who is particularly well-known for his portrait of Barack Obama.

Wiley's paintings are realistic and often have poses mimicking traditional European portraits. He contrasts this with highly decorated backgrounds inspired by textiles, wallpaper or nature — for example, Obama is surrounded by blooming green plants here.

Create your own portrait in the style of Kehinde Wiley

1. Look around the gallery or online at some portraits. Choose your favourite pose and an artwork that would make an interesting background, maybe something colourful or patterned so it will really stand out. Take photographs **if you're allowed,** or scribble them down in your sketchbook so that you remember them.

2. When you get home, get a friend or family member to pose like the picture you chose in the gallery. Draw them, either from life or from a photograph. Make sure you leave plenty of space around them for the background.

3. Copy the background you found in the gallery. You could use a different material to add extra contrast — for example, you might use paint for your portrait and then use collage for the background.

4. Finally, decorate the frame around your subject — the fancier the better!

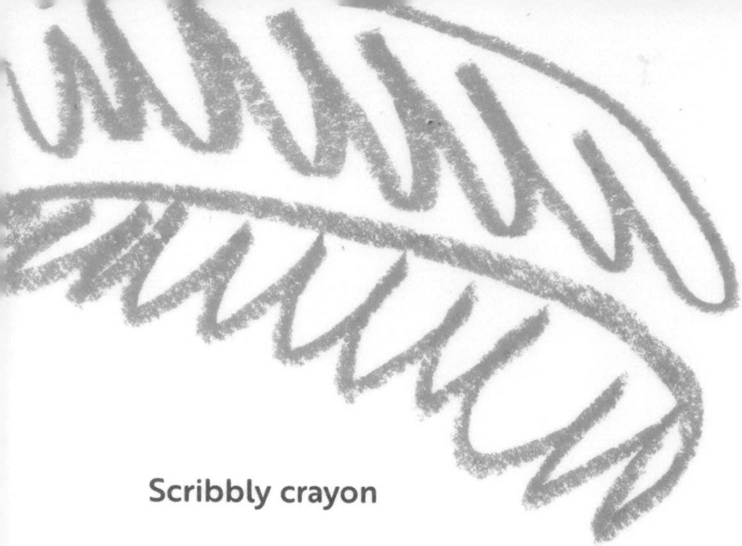

Scribbly crayon

A walk in the park

Nature is full of exciting and surprising things that are just waiting to be discovered. Something as small as a mark on a leaf or as big as the shape of a tree could inspire your next great piece of art. This chapter is packed with activities for you to do in a park, the countryside or in your garden, if you have one.

Soft watercolour

Squiggles and swirls

Here are some marks and materials you can use to represent nature. What other marks can you think of?

Fuzzy felt tip pen

Add some more marks to this page

Spiky pencil lines

Collage

Dashes and lines

Using some of the techniques on the previous page, fill this spread
with all the plants, trees, flowers and insects that you can see.
The more full you make this page the better!

Tip!
Start your drawing
with lighter colours and
materials, and then try
layering darker line work
on top of this.

Bingo!

Fill out these bingo cards at your favourite park. When you see somebody or something that matches the description, do a quick drawing in the box.

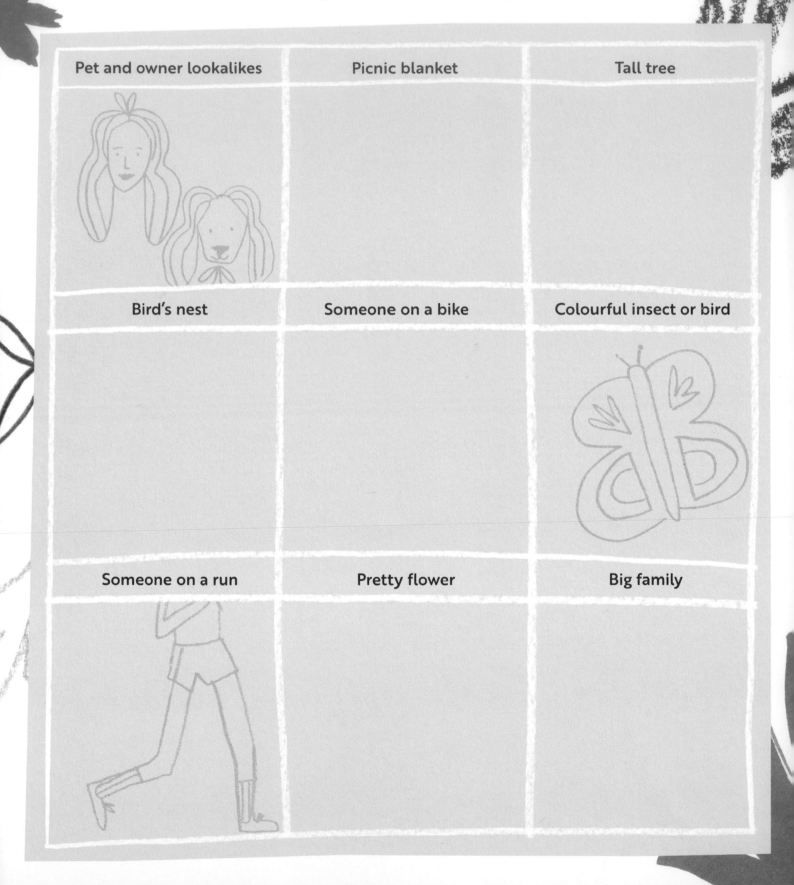

Pet and owner lookalikes	Picnic blanket	Tall tree
Bird's nest	**Someone on a bike**	**Colourful insect or bird**
Someone on a run	**Pretty flower**	**Big family**

Create your own categories for more games of bingo

Describe some of the plants and trees around you
What colours, shapes and patterns are they? Are the branches leafy or bare?
Are they moving in the wind?

Look down

What's on the ground? Is there green grass, pebbles or mud? Can you see any fallen leaves or wiggling worms? Are there any flowers growing from the soil?

Look up

What can you see above you? The branches of tall trees? A blue sky with fluffy clouds? A flock of birds or the trail of an airplane?

Henry Moore

1898–1986

Henry Moore was a British sculptor. A sculptor is an artist who works with materials to create 3D pieces of art. Many of Moore's sculptures are of the human body, and nature had a big influence on the shapes he would use in his work. Moore would collect rocks, shells, stones and even old animal bones, and he used these as inspiration for some of his sculptures.

Design a Henry Moore-style sculpture

Find a selection of sticks and stones with some interesting shapes and textures. Try and arrange them in a way that reminds you of a human or an animal, and use that as inspiration to draw your sculpture below.

Take some time to look closely at one plant. Draw it here

Draw a close up of one of its leaves

If it has flowers, draw one here

**Do you know what this plant is called?
If not, make up a new name for it**

Georgia O'Keeffe

1887–1986

Georgia O'Keeffe was an American painter, best known for her close-up paintings of flowers. She wanted to show people all the details and beauty that she saw in flowers, so rather than painting them at their real size, she zoomed right in and painted huge versions of them.

Georgia O'Keeffe wanted to surprise even busy New Yorkers into seeing flowers afresh

Create your own Georgia O'Keeffe-inspired drawing

Look really closely at a flower. Is there a particular part of it that is the most interesting to you? Draw a BIG version of it here, making sure to fill the page and include as much detail as you can.

Tip!
You could also do your drawing from a very zoomed-in photo of a flower.

Henri Matisse

1869–1954

Henri Matisse was a French artist. For most of his life he painted people, landscapes and still lifes. When he grew older and wasn't able to paint as much, he began working in collage. A collage is a piece of art made from sticking different materials (like paper or fabric) to a surface. To make his collages, Matisse would paint large sheets of paper in vibrant colours and cut shapes from them.

Collage is a great technique to experiment with as you can focus on the shapes of an object rather than the detail within it. You can also play around with colour and exciting compositions. It can be a fantastic way to loosen up and create fun, lively images.

Leaves are a useful place to start looking for interesting forms to collage as they come in all kinds of shapes and sizes. They can be big or small, round or pointy, wiggly or spiky! Have a look around for some interestingly-shaped leaves, and collect the most exciting ones.

Stick in some leaves or draw around them

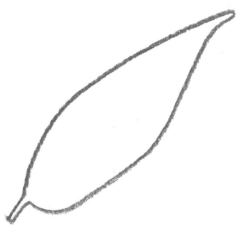

Get some coloured paper (or if you really want to unleash your inner Matisse, paint some sheets yourself) and some scissors. Using the leaves you have collected or drawn around on the previous page as your inspiration, cut out shapes from the coloured paper. Play around with different colours and sizes.

When you are happy with the shapes, arrange them in different ways on the page on the right, and stick down your favourite composition.

Some ideas for compositions

Ordered

Simplistic

Symmetrical

Size order

Create your collage here

Signed, sealed, delivered

On holiday, you might have sent a postcard to a friend or your family. Sending a postcard is lovely for the recipient, but can also be a great way to reflect on your surroundings or write about them, and you don't have to be on holiday to do this!

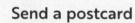

Send a postcard

On the right are some postcards for you to cut out or copy. Next time you go on a walk, to a museum, or even to the shops, write and design a postcard to send to a friend. What would you like to show or tell them about your surroundings?

GREETINGS FROM _____

GREETINGS FROM _____

GREETINGS FROM _____

GREETINGS FROM _____

Here are some extra activities you can do at home!

Draw the view out of your bedroom window
using only three colours

Draw something in your kitchen
using the continuous line technique

Look up at the clouds and create a collage
inspired by the shapes you see

Paint something from whatever's
on TV right now

Draw a portrait of one of the artists
in this book

Look out for accidental faces in places and objects and
photograph them

Look at one of your existing drawings through a finder, and
create a new composition inspired by what you see

Hopefully this book has got your creative juices
flowing and you have learnt some new ways to
look at the world!

Remember to keep being curious about
everything that catches your eye —
if you look, you can find inspiration
for your art all around you.

**Keep looking, keep seeing,
and keep creating!**

– Lucia